Which Side of Your Brain Am I Talking To?

The Advantages of Using Both Sides Of Your Brain!

左脳と右脳両脳 を使用した時の利点

Boyé Lafayette De Mente

***

Why Women Must Use the Less-Dominant Side of Their Brains in Order to Survive!

***

Phoenix Books / Publishers
Phoenix / Tokyo

ISBN: 0-914778-95-1

editor@phoenixbookspublishers.com

Copyright 2005 by Boyé Lafayette De Mente.

Other Books by the Author

Japanese Etiquette & Ethics in Business
Visitor's Guide to Arizona's Indian Reservations
Korean Etiquette & Ethics in Business
Korean in Plain English
Japanese in Plain English
Chinese Etiquette & Ethics in Business
Businessman's Quick-Guide to Japan
Survival Japanese
Japan Made Easy—All You Need to Know to Enjoy Japan
Etiquette Guide to Japan
Instant Japanese
Japan's Cultural Code Words
Chinese in Plain English
China's Cultural Code Words
Mexican Cultural Code Words
Mexican Etiquette & Ethics in Business
Korea's Business & Cultural Code Words
Korean Business Etiquette
There is a Word for it in Mexico
KATA—The Key to Understanding & Dealing With the Japanese
Asian Face Reading
The Japanese Samurai Code: Classic Strategies for Success
Samurai Strategies—41 Keys to Success from Musashi Miyamoto's "Book of Five Rings"
Cultural Code Words of the Hopi People
Cultural Code Words of the Navajo People
Instant Chinese
Survival Chinese
Instant Korean
Survival Korean
Japan Unmasked—The Culture & Character of the Japanese
The Secrets of Japanese Design

CONTENTS

Preface:

Which Side of Your Brain Am I Talking To?
Cross-Over between Brains /
Male & Female Differences
Cultural Differences

[I]

The Japanese Language Factor 11

[II]

Dual-Brained Japan 14

[III]

The Impact of the Emotional Factor
On Japanese Culture 17

[IV]

Fuzzy Thinking vs. Linear Thinking 19

[V]

Emotions vs. Reason 23

[VI]

Intuition vs. Reason 27

[VII]

Etiquette vs. Disharmony 30

[VIII]

Policies vs. Principles 32

[IX]

Aestheticism vs. Practicality 33

[X]

Conformism vs. Entrepreneurship 37

[XI]

Feminine vs. Masculine 40

[XII]

Humanism vs. Scientism 43

[XIII]

Groupism vs. Individualism 46

[XIV]

Harmony vs. Reality 49

[XV]
Passivity vs. Aggressiveness 52

[XVI]
Spirit vs. Reality 54

[XVII]
Quality vs. Profit 56

[XVIII]
Diligence vs. Getting By 60

[XIX]
Risk-Aversion vs. Risk-Taking 63

[XX]
Sincerity vs. Insincerity 65

[XXI]
Wet vs. Dry 67

[XXII]
Dual-Brain Views
That Distinguish the Japanese 70

Aesthetics 70

Apparel 72
Art 74
Beauty 75
Bathing 77
Business Management 78
Bragging 80
Cuteness 81
Decision-Making 82
Etiquette 83
Flattery 84
Humility 85
Intelligence 87
Mental Health 88
Problem Solving 89
Self-Respect 91
Sex 92
Shame 93
Spirituality 94
Style 95
Summary 96

Preface:

Which Side of Your Brain Am I Talking To?

IT has been proven beyond a reasonable doubt that there are basic differences in the functioning of the left and right sides of the brain.

Scientists tell us that the left sphere of the brain is programmed for linear or straight-line thinking, and is "in charge" of routine, repetitive physical actions, for the use of logic, for direct verbal communication, and for making objective fact-based decisions, etc.

The right side of the brain, on the other hand, is said to be more concerned with the emotions, personal relationships and aesthetics.

Cross-Over between Brains

Obviously, there is considerable cross-over between the two sides of the brain, but the basic functions of its two sides are different, resulting in people acting and reacting differently, depending on which side of the brain is engaged.

It is generally accepted that the right side of the brain is normally engaged when contemplating and discussing matters of religion, aesthetics, and other subjects not based on hard, objective facts—and this is, of course, why such discussions tend to become very emotional.

Still, many people also engage the left side of their brain when discussing these topics in an effort to explain them logically—to make them more convincing.

It is also generally accepted that the left side of the brain is engaged when thinking about and pursuing such matters as engineering, math and scientific research. A degree of emotional thinking is probably unavoidable, but people engaged in these pursuits tend to keep their emotions locked away in the right sides of their brains.

Male & Female Differences

There are significant differences in the functioning of male and female brains. Women are genetically programmed to be more right-brain oriented than men. They are naturally more emotional, more caring, more nurturing, and more aesthetically inclined than men.

However, despite the fact that women are inherently more emotional than men, they have been forced from the beginning to develop their ability to think and act in rational, practical ways in order to survive and perpetuate the species. In some respects, this makes women superior to men.

In other words, women in *left-brain* oriented cultures are generally forced to rely on their *right-brain* orientation (the emotional side) for survival and success. This often means using their sexuality both offensively and defensively. [The U.S. is a good example of this syndrome.]

In contrast to this, women in *right-brain* oriented cultures are generally forced to develop their *left-brain* abilities in order to survive in male-dominated societies, with the result that they are typically more rational and more practical than their right-brain oriented men folk. [Mexico is a good example of this syndrome.]

Cultural Differences
Some cultures are mostly left-brain centered, while others are more right-brain centered. Among the left-brain oriented cultures, the most prominent include China, the United States, Germany, England, Russia and Israel.

The cultures of all Spanish speaking countries, as well as France and Italy, are combinations of left-brain and right-brain thinking and behavior, with the right-brain often taking the lead.

In the "war" between the two sides of the brain Japan is unique.

According to prominent Japanese "brain authority," Dr. Tadanobu Tsunoda, the Japanese process *both* logical and emotional thoughts on the *left* sides of their brains.

Dr. Tsunoda presents evidence that it is the nature of the Japanese language which results in the Japanese processing both logical and emotional information on the left sides of their brains.

And it is my contention that this multiple use of the left side of the brain by the Japanese is the source of many of their most positive cultural traits, and played a major role in their being able to transform tiny, resource-poor Japan into an economic superpower.

This book identifies those traits, and suggests how people in the rest of the world could make more efficient—and more humane—use of both sides of their brains.

Boyé Lafayette De Mente

[I]
The Japanese Language Factor

JAPAN'S Dr. Tadanobu Tsunoda, noted author of *The Japanese Brain* who began as an audiologist and otologist, learned during decades of research that there is a fundamental difference in the hemispheric dominance in the brains of Japanese and non-Japanese.

Dr. Tsunoda discovered that the Japanese process both logical information and emotional information on the left sides of their brains, while non-Japanese divide these two functions between the left and right sides, processing logical thoughts with the left sides of their brains and emotional thoughts with the right sides.

Further research by Dr. Tsunoda demonstrated that this difference in brain dominance is a direct result of the native language of each individual. What was even more remarkable is that he found that only two languages, Japanese and Polynesian, *always* result in the speakers processing *both* emotional and logical information in the left sides of their brains.

Dr. Tsunoda learned that the secret of which side of the brain is used to process sounds is based on whether or not the sounds are harmonic or non-harmonic. The left side of the brain processes non-harmonic sounds; the right side processes harmonic sounds.

He also discovered that the combination of vowels and consonants in the Japanese language results in the brain stem automatically switching their emotional reactions, as well as their language processing, to the left side of their brains.

Dr. Tsunoda reconfirmed that in non-Japanese speakers the left side of the brain is dominate in logic and calculation, and the right side of the brain is dominate in the expression of emotions, the recognition of shapes, responding to natural sounds, and thought processes pertaining to analogy.

In another surprise, Dr. Tsunoda found that the sounds produced by Western musical instruments are processed by the *right side* of the brain, and sounds produced by Japanese musical instruments are processed by the *left side* of the brain.

On the surface, this might appear to be a contradiction, but the answer lies in the fact that music produced by Japanese instruments is non-harmonic, while that produced by Western instruments is harmonic—reinforcing Dr. Tsunoda's findings that the left side of the brain processes non-harmonic sounds while the right side of the brain processes harmonic sounds.

In his experiments, Dr. Tsunoda learned that the switching between the two brain hemispheres occurs primarily in the brain stem, located under the cortex, which divides the brain into the harmonic brain (the right side), and the non-harmonic brain (the left side).

He also determined that this switching process is hard-wired into the brain by the time an individual is nine years old as a direct result of exposure to speech sounds, and that speech sounds are automatically switched to the left side of the brain.

He says that the switching of sounds between the two sides of the brain appears to be related to their frequencies as measured in hertz.

Another interesting result of his experiments was that sexual behavior is processed by the right side of the brain, the emotional side—which obviously accounts for all of the irrational behavior of men and women when it comes to sex.*

---

*Science has shown that feelings of *happiness* are centered in the *left* side of the brain, which appears to be at odds with the traditional left-brain behavior of the Japanese, since they did not treat happiness as a right or as a goal to pursue for its own sake. Latin Americans, on the other hand, rank as among the happiest people on the planet, regardless of their economic and social situation—a phenomenon that is apparently based on the fact that they are culturally conditioned to emphasize the sunny side of life. Japanese, on the other hand, traditionally emphasized the impermanence and sadness of life—a mindset that the younger generations of Japanese have left behind.

Dr. Tsunoda's experiments proved that the difference between Japanese and non-Japanese in brain dominance is purely environmental, and is not related to race in any way. He tested Japanese-Americans who had been raised in the U.S., and found that like other non-Japanese they processed emotions on the right side of their brains.

Another of the more intriguing results suggested by Dr. Tsunoda's research is that cosmic activity, the rotation of the earth and lunar motion, etc., appears to have an influence on the switching between the left and right sides of the brain.

He says this suggests a sub-cortical biological function that could go back to the earliest days when mankind was much closer to nature and could probably feel the connection with the earth and the cosmos, as birds and animals appear to do.

[II]
Dual-Brained Japan

AS the world's only large, prominent group of people whose brains are programmed to deal with both emotional and logical information on their left sides, the Japanese are both unique and in a unique position. Their dual-brain orientation is the primary source of their most attractive and positive cultural traits as well as traits that are negative and often seriously disadvantageous, especially when they interact with purely left-brain oriented people.

One of the most positive cultural traits that the Japanese inherited from the influence of their language is the ability to apply both right and left-brain insight and energy in all of their efforts. This is a major advantage in many areas of life, and especially so in research and design activities.

One of the most negative elements that derive from the extraordinary emotional content of Japan's culture is that it makes it difficult and time-consuming for the Japanese to maintain harmonious relationships among themselves. It can be even more difficult for them to create and sustain good relations with people whose cultures are less emotion laden, because their priorities and goals are often different.

The government-sponsored industrialization of Japan between 1870 and 1890 required left-brain decision-making and a growing degree of left-brain behavior at the expense of right-brain facets of the country's traditional culture.

The introduction of democracy into Japan by the United States in 1945/6, and by the ongoing massive importation of popular American culture since then, have further eroded the day-to-day role of its right-brain culture.

But this erosion process did not penetrate to the core of the mindset or psyche of the Japanese because the Japanese language has remained virtually intact, and continues to program their emotional responses into the left side of their brains.

Another primary factor in the Japanese thinking process has been the widespread study and use of the English language since the mid-1900s—a strictly left-brain function that puts a special burden on the Japanese because they cannot separate the language from the emotional programming of the left-side of their brains.

Naturally enough, until the English-speaking Japanese achieve a certain level of fluency, it does not "feel" right, and in some instances, in business and other areas, what is said in English may not be regarded as official or binding. The Japanese also find prolonged listening to and speaking in English exceptionally tiring.

The benefits of English language study and use in Japan are, however, enormous. Despite the emotional conflict it causes, it nevertheless programs them to think and speak in more logical, more concrete, more precise terms that are culturally taboo when they are expressed in Japanese.

There is still another positive side to the Japanese being required to learn English (or any other foreign language)—if they begin the study in early childhood. Brain research indicates that people who are bilingual from a young age are less likely to suffer age-related mental decline as they get older.

The scientists say this beneficial affect probably results from the fact that the brain has to work harder to handle two (or more!) languages, and this exercise keeps its neural pathways in better shape.

For the foreseeable future, the core of Japanese culture is going to remain dual-brained, which, as it turns out in the increasingly global world, is an advantage.

[III]
Impact of the Emotional Factor On Japanese Culture

DUAL-BRAIN dominance in Japanese culture has been profound, influencing every aspect of their deepest values, their motivations, and their day-to-day thinking and behavior. This influence is especially visible in their arts and crafts, and in everything else that is normally described as being *Japanese*, including in the way they go about such mundane things as arranging food on a plate.

The role and influence of most of the physical manifestations of the dual-brain dominance in Japanese culture are positive, and account for virtually all of the things that both Japanese and non-Japanese find so attractive and so emotionally and spiritually satisfying.

In one very real sense, the physical manifestations of Japan's dual-brain dominant culture are "neutral" in that the emotional or aesthetic reaction they elicit from viewers is a personal, private thing. In those who are aesthetically attuned, viewing these things results in a variety of pleasant feelings that are sensual in nature.

However, in all of the areas of Japanese life that involve intangible facets of the culture, everything that comes under the heading of attitudes and behavior is directly and immediately impacted by the emotional factor, and this impact is frequently negative.

When the Japanese are dealing with other Japanese, and all are on the same cultural channel, the aspects of their emotional orientation that conflict with characteristic left-brain attitudes and behavior are generally kept under control by a variety of institutionalized forms of communication, tolerance, and cooperation.

By the same token, when the Japanese are dealing with people whose left-brains are dominate and who have not been culturally programmed to accommodate emotional thinking and behavior, misunderstandings and some measure of friction are inevitable—especially when the left-brain oriented people concerned are not sensitive to cultural differences, or choose to ignore them.

Since the late 1800s, many Japanese have been forced to become acutely aware that their values and behavior often differ markedly from those of foreigners—especially Westerners—but just knowing that the differences exist does not mean that they are easy to overcome, especially when both sides have been programmed to believe that their way is the best way.

In most of their international dealings, the Japanese have been forced to be the first and sometimes the only ones to alter their way of doing things in order to succeed in business and political affairs.

The lines between right-brain thinking and behaveing and left-brain thinking and behaving are not always clear and cross-thinking and behaving is common. In many areas of business and in professional and social relationships these differences are pronounced enough that they can be quantified, making it possible for people who are aware of them to adjust their thinking and behavior to accommodate the differences.

At the same time, there are many areas of behavior in which the typical dual-brain approach of the Japanese contrasts sharply with the left-brain approach of non-Japanese but ends up being an advantage for the Japanese.

[IV]
Fuzzy Thinking
Vs.
Linear Thinking

THE "mother" element in the Japanese way of thinking is what I call "fuzzy thinking," or "holistic thinking," which often contrasts sharply with the linear way most of the rest of the world thinks.

This supposition is based in part on the observable way the Japanese think and behave, and in part on the theory of Dr. Tsunoda. As noted, the Japanese are literally programmed to combine emotional and logical thinking in a "left-brain way" that makes them virtually unique in the world, despite their cultural kinship with Koreans and Chinese.

While there are a number of similarities in the traditional cultures of the Japanese, Koreans and Chinese, these similarities came about because primitive Korea and then primitive Japan adopted many facets of Chinese culture very early in their histories.

And while these cultural imports from China included virtually all of the arts and crafts that came to be associated with Korea and Japan—along with the very sophisticated Chinese way of writing, as well as the form of government, Buddhism, Confucianism and Taoism—both Korea and Japan retained their own cultural essence that made them different from the Chinese.

In the case of Japan, the cultural factor that made the Japanese different in the first place and prevented them from becoming total clones of the Chinese was, according to Dr. Tsunoda's theory, the influence of the Japanese language that makes the left sides of their brains dominant in both emotional and logical thinking.

While there are some who dispute Dr. Tsunoda's theory, there can be no disputing the proposition that the Japanese think and behave differently, because these differences can be readily observed and deduced.

Even a cursory study of Japan's traditional culture, especially after the emergence of the samurai class from 1192 on, clearly demonstrates that the Japanese were perfectly capable of thinking in linear terms when it came to structuring and enforcing the new shogunate form of government.

But in implementing and maintaining this form of government, and in going about the daily affairs of living and working, the Japanese were significantly influenced by the emotional elements of their culture.

This normally right-brain influence was manifested in their approach to arts and crafts, in their architecture, in designing their gardens, in their emphasis on aesthetic practices, in their extraordinary attachment to poetry, and in their overall view of nature.

In fact, the influence of the emotional side of their culture was so powerful that the Japanese developed an aversion to thinking that was based solely on facts and logic. They regarded this way of thinking as callous, cruel and anti-human. The attribute they most admired in people was "humanism."

Japanese contact with the left-brained oriented Western world, first in the 16th century, and then again in the mid 1800s, was to have profound consequences for both sides. Japan's emotion oriented culture clashed with the logic-centered cultures of the West.

But there was early evidence that the holistic way of thinking that was more characteristic of the Japanese than it was of Westerners was going to give them a special advantage in the future.

One of the most telling demonstrations of this advantage occurred when the U.S.'s Commodore Perry arrived in Japan in 1853 to force the country to open its doors to the outside world.

Perry and his men went ashore at the small fishing village of Shimoda at the end of Izu Peninsula, well south of the Shogunate headquarters in Edo (Tokyo). Perry presented the samurai delegation of the local lord with a miniature train that was powered by steam.

The Japanese had never seen a train before. They took it away and three days later came back with several suggestions for improving its technology.

Within a few decades the Japanese had demonstrated an extraordinary ability to understand, duplicate and improve on the technology of a wide range of Western imports. And despite some foreign views to the contrary, the Japanese were soon to prove that they were also capable of basic research leading to new technology.

Following the debacle of Japan's attempt to conquer East Asia, Southeast Asia and the islands of the Pacific, their ability to absorb, improve on and innovate technology played a key role in their quick emergence as the second largest economy in the world—an absolutely incredible phenomenon that many Westerners still have difficulty understanding and accepting.

The natural tendency of the Japanese to look at all things from a holistic viewpoint continues to be a valuable asset, especially in the use of technology and aesthetic factors that do not directly threaten the entrenched bureaucracies of business and government.

There are, however, negative elements in the dulbrain orientation of the Japanese that have continued to plague them, often making them feel and act like fish out of water. This includes an ongoing discomfort with un-adorned logical thinking, quick decision-making, and dealing on a level playing field with left-brain thinkers.

However, the more experienced the Japanese become at cross-over thinking, the more the negative influences of their emotional orientation will diminish, and the more they will gain from being able to view things holistically.

The Japanese are well aware of the fact that there is a fundamental difference in the way they think and the way others think, and this has resulted in them being virtually obsessed with these differences, turning the study and writing about them into a major industry. More than one theory has been advanced to explain these differences.

Rather than using the right-brain left-brain theory to explain these differences, Prof. Michinobu Kato, author of *Watakushi-tachi no Nihonjin Ron*, or *Our Japanology,* and other works, describes the Japanese as analog thinkers and others as digital thinkers. He says—wrongly, I believe—that this is the reason the Japanese typically are not good at theory or abstract thinking. [With both civil and culture restraints removed, theoretical and abstract thinking are flourishing in Japan.]

Prof. Kato goes on to say that the Japanese are not good at dealing with matters of high finance and Western style management, suggesting that their analog thinking limits the depth and scope of their thinking. He adds, however, that the Japanese are exceptionally good at dealing with practical, concrete matters such as manufacturing and building things because they do not require logical debate.

[V]
Emotions vs. Reason

LONG before I had ever heard of Dr. Tadanobu Tsunoda's theory of the Japanese being dual-brain oriented I had written extensively about the emotional content of the Japanese mindset and Japanese culture.

I noted in one of my earlier books that Westerners who go to Japan for business purposes—or take up residence there for any purpose—and come face-to-face with typical Japanese behavior are inevitably surprised and often frustrated by instances when emotion rather than reason determines the actions and reactions of the Japanese.

I also noted that nothing was more irritating to the logical-minded Westerner than becoming involved with people who do not behave in a "reasonable" manner—much less encountering a whole nation of "unreasonable" people.

As it turned out, however, the Japanese actually have a dual mindset made up of a combination of emotional intelligence and reasoning power. And when this dual mindset is brought to bear in combination, it gives them extra insight, which they call *kansei* (kahn-say-ee) or "emotional rightness" and use in reference to how people perceive, react to, and use products.

Kansei may also be translated as "absolute awareness," in which case it refers to the emotional and rational content of a product—and is an insight, or skill, that the Japanese have in abundance.

In addition to deliberately building *kansei* into their products, the Japanese also infuse it into their advertising campaigns, generally giving it more priority than the utilitarian value of the product.

The many wonderful aesthetic elements in Japan's traditional arts and crafts are among the positive manifestations of the emotional orientation of the people.

Japan's traditional human-centered emotional approach to business management was a rational and humane way of doing things, and it worked exceedingly well until Western style competition, internationally as well as domestically, made it disadvantageous.

Now that the Japanese have become dependent upon foreign economic and political relationships with people who are mostly left-brain oriented, the emotional factor in their makeup can be a serious handicap or an advantage, depending on their awareness of the factor and their experience in using or suppressing it.

Their relationships with less emotional people can become even more complicated when the foreign side refuses to compromise, or becomes extreme. Some non-Japanese are able to manage emotional factors better than others, while many Westerners, Americans in particular, often appear to have few insights or skills in dealing with emotional situations.

Until the last decades of the 20th century, most of the burden of dealing with the emotional content that the Japanese brought to foreign business relationships was placed on their shoulders by default. However, by the end of the century, most Westerners doing business in and with Japan had become aware of the cultural differences, and had learned how to accommodate them to some degree.

At the same time, the Japanese who are involved in international affairs are becoming more experienced and more skilled in managing the emotional factors that remain integral elements of their culture, and in assuming a more rational approach in their efforts. The more English they learn the easier this challenge becomes, since it is virtually "culture free" and when using it they do not have to speak with the ambiguity that is built into the Japanese language.

However, this facility in English sometimes results in problems developing afterward. The foreign listener naturally takes the speaker at his or her word—his or her *English* word, that is—only to discover later that this assumption is misplaced.

It often happens in business, diplomatic and other situations that Japanese will make statements and/or commitments in English that either do not reflect their real positions, or are not acceptable by the group or organization they represent.

The Left-Brain Right-Brain Factor in Human Behavior / 27

Whether or not these statements and positions by people speaking in English are meant to be devious or deceitful, or merely express what the Japanese believes the foreign listener wants to hear without any intention of doing harm, depends on the situation.

The Japanese are very experienced at dealing with ambiguous speech that can be take in different ways, since it is a characteristic of the Japanese language and a key factor in their intellectual conditioning. They naturally leave it up to the other party to divine what they really mean or the nature of the real situation.

This cultural habit sometimes carries over into their use of English or other foreign languages, since there is the built-in mindset that what they say directly is *tatemae* (tah-tay-my), or a façade to draw the other person out and maintain harmony; not their *honne* (hone-nay), their real thoughts or intentions.

In other words, the emotional content in the character of the Japanese is not the only factor that influences their attitudes and behavior. The influence of the ambiguity of the Japanese language, which is built into the language to help ensure harmony in all relationships, also plays an important role in their day-to-day relationships with other Japanese as well as non-Japanese.

Here too, the Japanese tendency to combine emotion with reason often turns out to be an advantage in their relationships with non-Japanese, because no matter how logic-oriented the foreign side may be, there is a part of them that wants and responds positively to the human (emotional) touch.

[VI]
Intuition vs. Reason

ONE of the most important of the cultural traits that the Japanese derived from their right-brain orientation was the practice of giving intuition precedence over reason, especially in very weighty affairs when the consequences were, or could be, enormous.

Japanese history is replete with incidents in which the fate of individuals, groups and even the nation itself hung in the balance, and the decisions made were based on intuition rather than reason. In fact, the higher placed and more powerful the individuals concerned in these situations, the more likely they were to depend on intuition rather than reason.

Stories about leading samurai of old and leading businessmen of the recent past, including the great Konosuke Matsushita, invariably include tales of their use of intuition as their primary source of wisdom and in the decisions they made.

There is a special word in the Japanese language that refers to this kind of decision-making. It is called *haragei* (hah-rah-gay-ee), which literally translates as "the art of the stomach"—a more elegant phrase than the Western "gut feeling."

Haragei refers to is the use of common cultural know-ledge to make decisions that are compatible with the mindset and spirit of the Japanese, and will therefore be accepted and acted on in the manner desired by all of those who are involved.

Haragei therefore equates to some extent with what I call "cultural telepathy"—that is, being able to communicate with people on the basis of common knowledge and common experience; although there is another, more precise, Japanese word for this form of resolving situations and making decisions: *chokkan* (choke-kahn), which translates as "intuition."

The reason why intuition has traditionally played such an important role in Japanese life is because the people were homogenized to an extraordinary degree by their programming in exactly the same beliefs and forms of behavior, and therefore thought and acted very much alike.

This meant that they could intuit what others were thinking and what they would probably do under most circumstances. It also meant that they "knew" what was right and wrong without having to reason it out because the "correct" opinion or reaction was common knowledge.

Present-day Japanese are far less homogenous than what they were as late as the 1970s and 80s, but the power of the traditional culture is still very much in evidence in the attitudes and behavior of older people. Most of the time it is still possible to assume that in group situations most of them will react in "the Japanese way"—that is, according to identifiable Japanese values that remain traditional to varying degrees.

One of the challenges in dealing effectively with Japanese in situations where the individual is a member of a group is being able to determine whether a reaction is based on intuition or reason. Among younger individuals reason now generally overrides intuition, except in group situations.

Generally, reactions that are based on intuition reflect the traditional Japanese mindset as a whole, while reactions based on pure reason may reflect the opinion or position of individuals, and not be binding on the group.

There is a great deal of "folk wisdom" in "Japanese intuition," and when that is combined with reason, it often results in a more comprehensive answer or solution to whatever discussion or problem is at hand.

Unfortunately, it often takes left-brained oriented people months to years before they come around to understanding and accepting the Japanese viewpoint.

[VII]
Etiquette vs. Disharmony

THE Japanese regard Americans as the most unpredictable people on the planet because we do not have a precise etiquette that everyone follows in speech or in physical behavior. In contrast, to our individualistic way of talking and behaving, the Japanese have traditionally behaved according to a strict, prescribed, uniform etiquette that was equated with morality and being civilized, and was perfectly predictable.

Japanese etiquette grew out of ritualistic behavior that was designed to show respect toward all of the spirits of nature, and was then refined and institutionalized in their daily lives by the influence of Buddhist and Confucian precepts that were imported from China.

The goal of Japanese etiquette was to ensure harmony—not only between them and the many gods of their pantheon, but among themselves—harmony that came to be based on absolute respect for parents, seniors, teachers, and those in positions of power.

The respect-etiquette system that developed in Japan was influenced in very specific and powerful ways by the emotional character of the people, which made them nature-oriented, harmony-oriented and compulsive about doing things in an orderly, ritualistic way.

The emotion-charged etiquette of the Japanese was not limited to behavior in social situations. It permeated their culture from top to bottom. Over the early centuries they developed precise ways of doing virtually everything in their daily existence, to the point that these ways were no longer regarded as arbitrary forms of etiquette. They became an integral part of their identity as Japanese.

The introduction of individualism, democracy and other cultural concepts from the West, which began wholesale in 1945 with the U.S. occupation of the country, has eroded the traditional etiquette of the Japanese, especially among the young. But it was so deeply embedded in the cultural and psyche of the people that much of it has survived and it is still characteristic of the majority of the Japanese in their daily behavior.

One of the characteristics of traditional Japanese etiquette that is still visible in Japan today is the smooth and harmonious way society continues to function as a whole, despite what amounts to a huge population in a very small land area.

This etiquette is conspicuously visible in homes, in stores, on the streets, in offices, in factories, and elsewhere.

Conforming to a high standard of etiquette may be intellectually driven to some degree, but it is primarily an emotional response to others, requiring that one suppress his or her ego and built-in selfishness on behalf of others.

The emotional left-brain orientation of the Japanese can therefore be credited with a style and level of etiquette that has distinguished them since ancient times, and has contributed enormously to the ambiance and efficiency of Japanese culture.

[VIII]
Policies vs. Principles

THE dual-brain orientation of Japan's traditional culture, combined with Buddhist, Confucian and Shinto influences, resulted in the culture becoming primarily human-centered rather than principle-centered.

This meant that many decisions in Japan that left-brain thinkers would make on the bases of objective principles were commonly made on the basis of human interests prevailing at that particular time and place.

The various influences on the Japanese process of thinking were so powerful that their lives were generally controlled by policies rather than principles. In fact, as late as the last decades of the 20th century, sociologists and others often complained, "We Japanese don't have principles; we have policies!"

In other words, the traditional, fundamental morality of the Japanese was circumstantial, or conditional, and was based on what the ruling power said it was. The day-to-day security and survival of the people depended upon them obeying the morality prescribed by those in power.

Until the introduction of democracy into Japan in 1945-46, behavior based on circumstances and policies rather than principles served Japan efficiently, if not well. In contests and other conflicts, those who do not have principles generally have an advantage.

There is now enormous economic, political and social pressure on Japan to conduct all of its affairs on the basis of well-established universal principles. And little by little, progress is being made. But a complete conversion to principle-based systems will take time. Such a fundamental change in a culture as powerful and as deeply entrenched as that of Japan is a generational thing.

Individually, most Japanese are as principled as any of their foreign counterparts may be, but generally speaking they must conform to the morality and policies of the systems they are in.

Still, it is not advisable for left-brained, principle-based, people to compromise their principles when dealing with the Japanese. The Japanese want to change the systems that control them, and often the only way they can do that is when outside pressure builds up to the point that a system-change becomes the only option.

Even in this area, one can find an advantage that the Japanese have when it comes to their view and use of policies. As a whole, the Japanese accept new, sensible policies quickly and completely, making it possible to implement new approaches virtually overnight—something that generally does not happen in logic-oriented societies where individualism and the freedom to debate anything and everything is the rule.

[IX]
Aestheticism vs. Practicality

THE traditional mindset of the Japanese was steeped in aestheticism as a result of the tenants of Shinto, their indigenous religion, because it was based on the worship of "nature spirits"—mountains and other high places, the sea, rain, rocks, trees, and other natural phenomena.

As the abode of spirits that controlled their survival and the quality of their lives, the Japanese treated flowers, milled lumber and building pillars, mountain peaks, scenic gorges and other manifestations of nature with ritual reverence, and became especially sensitive and respectful toward their natural beauty.

This cultural-induced sensitivity to and respect for the beauty of nature led the Japanese to strive to re-create the beauty of nature in their arts and crafts. This striving to recreate nature, combined with the master-apprentice approach to transmitting manual skills from one generation to the next, resulted in the quality of their crafts rising to the level of fine arts, reinforcing the role and importance of aesthetics in their lives.

But the Japanese did not stop there. Virtually all Japanese wrote poetry celebrating the beauty of nature. Skill in composing poetry was regarded as a measure of one's cultural achievements and morality. Outstanding poets won honor and lasting fame.

The Japanese went further in appreciating beauty and in exercising their aesthetic capabilities. They created a number of rituals that were specifically designed for communing with the beauty and spirits of nature.

These rituals included the famous tea ceremony, flower-viewing, moon-viewing, and snow-viewing. They were not just casual practices that one did now and then for relaxation. They were an important part of the cultural activities of the population.

The tea ceremony in particular, which was designed to demonstrate one's "cultural morality" and to soothe the spirit and purify the soul, became an essential part of the Japanese way of expressing their Japaneseness.

From the early 1600s until the beginning of modern times, Japan's famous samurai class spent as much time and as much energy developing their aesthetic prowess as they did honing their skill in the fighting arts.

The warrior who could not compose a poem, even under the most extreme conditions such as his imminent death, or conduct a tea ceremony with masterful grace, was considered uncultured and incomplete.

With the appearance of an affluent middle class of business people from the mid-1600s on, merchants vied with fief lords, members of the Shogun's court in Edo, and the Imperial Court in Kyoto in staging tea ceremonies—the largest of which had several hundred guests.

The unique tea ceremony and flower-viewing have survived into modern times, and continue to play a significant role in Japanese life. Both have many schools and large followings. Each spring virtually all Japanese in the country, from teenagers to the most elderly, participate in parties to celebrate the beauty of cherry blossoms.

While the aesthetic sense of the Japanese has given them a built-in advantage in business—from the design of products to packaging, displays and advertising—the emotional content of aestheticism, which is normally a right-brain thing, often becomes a negative factor in their conduct of business, diplomatic and political affairs.

On one occasion that I recall vividly, I experienced what then was a surprising example of the hold that aestheticism has on the Japanese mind. I was interviewing a company about a new product it had just released, but was unable to get the details needed for a story. The spokesperson kept asking me to comment on the "warm feelings" imparted by pebbles in a lobby fountain.

The aesthetic side of the Japanese character encompasses a deep-seated sense of harmony in all things, particularly in interpersonal relationships. This complicates their interacting with each other, and can be especially disadvantageous in their dealings with Westerners and other people who are not as emotion-bound and, in fact, try to separate personal feelings from their professional dealings.

Americans in particular are culturally conditioned to "grow up" and conduct their affairs in an objective, non-emotional manner—a factor that runs counter to the traditional Japanese way.

Since the Japanese must do business with the left-brain world, they are typically forced to suppress their emotional impulses, and often to downplay or forget altogether their right-brain skills. The fact that they have been able create an economic superpower is testimony to their perseverance and ability to use both sides of their brain when pride, honor and ambition are at stake.

I suggest that left-brain oriented people would be much better off if they consciously and deliberately adopted more practices and customs that would help develop the right side of their brains.

[X]
Conformism vs. Entrepreneurship

UNTIL 1945-47 when democratic principles were introduced into Japan by and from the United States, the Japanese were constrained by both custom and law from behaving as individuals. For more than a thousand years they had been physically programmed and mentally conditioned to conform to a precise etiquette and to an equally precise set of rules that controlled what they did and how they did it.

Throughout Japan's early history entrepreneurship, as it was exhibited in the West from the beginning of the Industrial Revolution, was suppressed. Until the end of Shogunate government in 1868, innovation, invention and even such practical things as building bridges across rivers was virtually banned.

A Shogunate proclamation that nothing new should be invented was aimed at maintaining the political and social status quo. The injunction against building bridges was a political measure to help prevent any of the 200-plus fief warlords from attacking the Shogunate head-quarters in Edo (Tokyo).

Throughout the history of the country, the right-brain/left-brain orientation of the Japanese, with all of its emotional and spiritual emphasis, was generally given precedence over other considerations. Conformism, down to the most routine forms of personal behavior, became the overwhelming rule in Japanese society.

Japanese who did not conform to the prescribed attitudes and behavior were in danger of losing their place in society, and in extreme cases their identity as Japanese. Behaving in a non-Japanese manner was not only regarded as disruptive, it was considered immoral.

Until the latter decades of the 20th century one of the elements of Japanese culture that was praised the highest was the virtually complete homogenization of the Japanese mindset and behavior.

The Japanese looked upon their homogeneity with enormous pride, and commonly pointed to it as one of their most important cultural traits, as well as a major economic and political advantage because it contributed significantly to wholehearted cooperation and mutual effort throughout society.

This, of course, was a very valid viewpoint until about 1970, by which time Japan was heavily involved in international trade and foreign affairs, popular American culture had begun to have a fundamental influence on the attitudes and behavior of the young, and millions of people had traveled abroad—all factors that had begun to build a desire for more individuality, more flexibility, and more non-Japanese spice in their lives.

During this decade, teenagers especially began to dress, talk and behave in ways that were absolutely unthinkable to their parents—to the point that sociologists began referring to them as *shinjinrui* (sheen-jeen-rooey), or "new breed of people."

When Japan's financial system tanked in 1990/1 and its amazing economic engine began to sputter, the cultural homogeneity and built-in imperative of conformity became major liabilities, resulting in a mental flip-flop, with leaders in virtually every field calling for more individuality, more entrepreneurship, in Japanese behavior.

Drastic and sometimes heroic steps were taken by many companies to change their corporate cultures to accommodate entrepreneurial behavior. But the older the company the more likely these changes could not occur within their existing frame-works, so their only choice was to establish wholly-owned subsidiaries, staff them with young people, and make them virtually autonomous from the parent companies.

However, the deep-seated power of the traditional culture combined with the ongoing influence of language-based dual-brain thinking has prevented the Japanese from totally changing their cultural and linguistic stripes, making the change from a conformist society to an entrepreneurial society a slow, incremental, generational process.

The more emphasis the Japanese put on learning foreign languages and the more adept they become at thinking outside of the Japanese box, the more advantage they will have from being able to tap into both sides of their brain.

There is growing evidence that Japanese born after 1980 are "bi-cultural" in the sense that they are able to use both sides of their brain with much more facility than the older generations—despite their original conditioning in emotion-based thinking.

[XI]
Feminine vs. Masculine

ONE of the more remarkable facets of Japanese culture is the fact that it is more feminine than masculine—a factor that plays a primary role in the positive affect it has on people; especially Westerners whose cultures are more masculine oriented.

The feminine nature of Japanese culture can be traced to the influence of Shinto, which is essentially based on the role and importance of fertility in all life, and, on the emotional content of the Japanese mindset, which is a product of their spiritual orientation.

Over the centuries much of the overall refinement of Japan's arts, crafts and lifestyle resulted from the feminine side of the culture. This feminine character had an especially profound influence on the shape, finish and aura of the arts, crafts and wearing apparel.

Still today, the feminine aspects of Japanese culture are obvious in the behavior of the people, in their aesthetic appreciation, in their emotional approach to relationships, in their emphasis on humanism, and in their preference for harmony and order in their lives.

The feminine side of Japan is especially conspicuous in girls and young women, who have traditionally radiated femininity on a much higher level than women in many other cultures—and this, of course, is the reason Western men have always found Japan especially attractive.

The feminine influence of Japanese culture has also traditionally been discernible in the character and behavior of Japanese men—from the wearing apparel to their stylized etiquette, not to mention their slight figures; all of which combined to result in Westerners underestimating them.

While the feminine qualities of Japan's culture today have been watered down by Western masculine influences, they remain strong enough to be visible and to have a powerful impact on virtually every aspect of life in the country.

The femininity of young Japanese women continues to draws Western men the way flame draws moths. The underlying feminine nature of Japanese things also acts as a magnet on Westerners, although this influence is mostly subconscious.

Interestingly, Western men are generally more comfortable in Japan than Western women—unless the women are into aesthetics and both consciously and subconsciously respond in a positive way to the feminine side of the culture.

However, the attraction that Japanese culture has for typical Western males is primarily sexual, not aesthetic. In fact, many Western men who stay in Japan for long periods of time because of the feminine appeal of the women and the sensual attraction of the culture—which is mostly subconscious—have a kind of love/hate relationship with the country. One might say they are held there against their will.

Overall, the influence of Japan's feminine culture is positive. It is the source of much of the cultural ambiance that makes life in the country so pleasing for most people. It also provides the Japanese with a number of assets that are advantageous in business—from the designing and manufacturing of products, to advertising, marketing and product displays in retail shops.

On the negative side, the dominant feminine nature of Japanese culture makes it difficult for the Japanese to deal with left-brain oriented cultures because they are more masculine, more direct, more "hard fact" oriented.

The influence of the more masculine Western cultures, particularly the culture of the United States, is gradually overlaying some of the aspects of the feminine side of Japanese culture but it is not likely to be eroded away any time soon.

In addition to being constantly renewed by the language, Japan's feminine culture is so deeply embedded in the psyche of the people that even without the influence of the language it would no doubt persist for many generations. And it should be recognized, celebrated and promoted for all of the benefits that it provides.

Just as the feminine nature of Japanese culture is an asset, the masculine nature of other cultures is often a major disadvantage to them—what one might call a cultural failure, at least as far as evolution is concerned. The male attributes that were useful before the advent of civilization are no longer needed, and yet the primitive masculine impulse to destroy and kill is still present in the male mind.

The answer to improving Japan's relationships with the rest of the world is not for the Japanese to wean themselves away from their feminine side, but for left-brain dominant people to add a feminine element to their cultures through education and practice in using the right side of their brains.

[XII]
Humanism vs. Scientism

INDUSTRIALIZATION was introduced into Japan in 1870 by a new crop of Japanese leaders who had defeated the feudal shogunate government and were determined to catch up with the West in terms of industrial and military power in order to avoid being colonized—and to prove the superiority of their culture.

Up to that time, the primary thrust of Japan's Shogunate government had been to maintain the status quo—politically, socially and economically—to prevent changes of any kind that would undermine its control of the country.

For the preceding 230-plus years this prevention took the form of isolating Japan from the rest of the world. In addition to this drastic political action, the Japanese had been culturally conditioned for close to a thousand years to revere the past, to look backward instead of forward.

These political and cultural factors emphasized humanism and downplayed or ignored altogether scientism and the natural sciences. Thus there had been very little innovation and invention in Japan up to that time.

The miniscule amount of modern science and technology that existed in Japan between the 1630s and the 1850s entered the country through a tiny crack that was left open to Dutch traders on a manmade islet in Nagasaki Bay. The islet was connected to the mainland by a narrow causeway blocked off by a huge gate that was guarded 24-hours a day by armed warriors.

Disinterest in scientific research was built into Japanese culture by an emphasis on the past, the importance of their emotional attachment to their ancient way of life, and the fact that such interest was blocked by the Shogunate government, which saw it as a major danger to its supremacy.

One of the more remarkable episodes in Japanese history was a decision by the Shogunate government in the 1600s to ban the use of guns [originally introduced into the country by Portuguese traders in 1543], as being "un-Japanese" and disruptive to the Japanese way of life.

Thus it came about that the humanism in Japanese culture took precedence over scientism until 1870, when the leaders of the new government set Japan on the left-brain path of industrialization and a Western-type economy.

As with so many other legacies of the traditional culture, humanism did not disappear from the scene when industrialization began. The new Western type businesses that were set up by the thousands were organized and managed according to right-brain humanistic precepts that had been a part of Japan's culture since day one.

Furthermore, the humanistic traditions of the Japanese did not prevent them from embracing scientism as soon as they were politically free to do so. From the 1870s on, thousands of Japanese began innovating and inventing with extraordinary enthusiasm and diligence.

This enthusiasm and diligence became even more pronounced following the end of World War II in 1945, and soon developed into an obsession that has continued to grow.

Despite this amazing switch to left-brain research, the Japanese did not give up their humanistic approach to management. As late as the 1980s, they took great pride in contrasting their humanistic approach to business with the "anti-human" policies and practices of American and other Western companies.

It was not until the "Big Bang" in the early 1990s when Japan's "bubble economy" suddenly began to lose power that the fabled humanism of the Japanese began to take a backseat to the left-brain management practices that included firing employees, closing factories and dispensing with the seniority-based system of wages.

One of the challenges the Japanese face now is not to lose all of their commitment to humanism in order to compete with other countries.*

---

*The traditional humanism of Japanese culture was a very selective thing, and was, in fact, often over-shadowed by a degree and level of inhumane behavior that, from a Western viewpoint, was unbelievably barbaric and cruel.

In the meantime, American, European and other Western companies have been under increasing pressure since the 1980s and 90s to humanize their management practices and many have done so successfully—a somewhat ironic switch from their left-brain way of doing things to a right-brain way of doing things.

It is a foregone conclusion that in the future Japanese style humanism will gradually assume more and more importance in the world, not only in business management but in all fields of endeavor, especially in science which now, more often than not, first serves the interest of military power before it gets down to the interest of the people.

[XIII]
Groupism vs. Individualism

FROM the dawn of their history the Japanese were encouraged, directed, and generally forced, to think and behave as groups rather than as individuals. In fact, during most of Japan's history individualistic behavior was not only considered immoral, it many situations it was against the law and could have fatal consequences.

One of the best-known Japanese proverbs notes that the person who stands out gets hammered down. Over the centuries this cultural imperative was so powerful that it was not until the 1990s, when the Japanese economy was shaken by a financial melt-down, that one began to hear calls for individualism, for entrepreneurship, and for "non-Japanese" thinking to get the economy back on an upward path.

During Japan's remarkable rise to economic superpowdom between 1945 and 1970, the social and corporation sanctions against individualistic behavior were very real and very harsh. People who were unusually intelligent or experienced and talented had to be extraordinarily careful not to bring the wrath of their co-workers down on them, or to be totally ignored or transferred to some meaningless job by their employers.

From 1960 until about 1990 thousands of individuals who had studied abroad to increase their technical skills and/or improve on their foreign language abilities—many of them actually sent abroad by their own companies—were treated as pariahs when they returned to Japan. Other thousands left Japan to take up research in other countries because their independent thinking and individualistic behavior was not tolerated by whatever company or organization they belonged to.

The fact that some of these individuals went on to achieve extraordinary success in their research [including winning Nobel Prizes] created a storm of criticism about the traditional social, economic and political sanctions against independent thinking and individualistic behavior.

These criticisms, combined with continuing concerns about Japan's economic future, resulted in weakening the anti-individualism mindset that had been drummed into the Japanese since ancient times, but it is still a major factor in every facet of Japanese life today and is not likely to disappear altogether in the foreseeable future.

The natural, native propensity of the Japanese to think and act as groups was significantly influenced by their right-brain orientation, which emphasizes human feelings and harmony in all relationships, and requires putting the group before the individual.

All of the religious and philosophical teachings that played a role in the creation of Japan's traditional culture, beginning with Shinto, and then including Buddhism and Confucianism, were also oriented toward group behavior and group responsibility.

Obviously, there is extraordinary merit in both individualism and groupism, either in combination or with each having its own time and place. A significant degree of Japan's extraordinary economic success between 1950 and 1990 was based on the ability of the people to work in groups in which harmony was virtually absolute.

But that was when Japan was still in a kind of time warp, operating under the same mindset that was forged during its long, mostly isolated, feudal period (1192-1868), and during which there was virtually no competition, domestically or internationally.

By 1980 economic changes that that had occurred worldwide had begun to seriously erode the benefits that had long accrued to Japan's exclusive group approach, and one began to hear appeals for more and more individualism and entrepreneurship.

While individualistic Americans are now striving to develop a more cooperative group-oriented culture, the Japanese are faced with the challenge of learning how to deal with and taken advantage of the power of individualism that is inherent in human nature.

But again, Japan's drive for individualism should not get so far out of hand that it replaces the power of working together and the cohesiveness that such cooperation brings to society—not to mention the fact that "group intelligence" is often more humane and more practical than individual intelligence.

Many of the greatest blunders in left-brain oriented societies have been the result of the beliefs and actions of individuals.

[XIV]
Harmony vs. Reality

THE harmony that was characteristic of Japanese society for most of the history of the country made it necessary for the people to suppress many of the traits that are inherent in all human beings, from egoism and personal interest to the fact that people are born with different temperaments.

But despite the homogeneity of the environment they grew up in the Japanese always ended up with different personalities.

The harmony that existed in pre-modern Japan was based in part on the cultural indoctrination they got from Shinto, Buddhism and Confucianism. But it was obedience to the laws of the Shogunate government that made this harmony the foundation of society. These laws, based on the samurai code of ethics that had been institutionalized and ritualized over the centuries, covered virtually every facet of behavior, and were strictly enforced. More often than not, the fate of lawbreakers was a quick death.

Generally speaking, harmony in pre-modern Japan took precedence over virtually all other considerations, which often made it necessary to suppress facts, the truth and especially human feelings. Duty and obligations came first, no matter what the personal consequences.

This cultural phenomenon gave birth to the custom of concealing the truth by speaking in ambiguous terms and by using the artifice described as *tatemae* (tah-tay-my) and *honne* (hone-nay), mentioned earlier.

Tatemae refers to a verbal façade that one presents as a front in order to avoid exposing one's *honne* or real intentions at the beginning of a dialogue or negotiation. The idea being that the dialogue will continue until both sides gradually reveal their true positions, without either side losing or gaining an advantage over the other, while maintaining carefully controlled harmony—a custom that is still characteristic of Japanese behavior today.

Not being aware of this cultural characteristic of Japanese behavior, the first Westerners in Japan in the 16th century often described them as habitual liars, unable to tell the truth. In fact, it was not until the last half of the 20th century that knowledge of this cultural trait became generally known to outsiders.*

---

*I introduced the *tatemae* and *honne* cultural factor to Western businessmen in my first book, *Japanese Etiquette & Ethics in Business*, published in 1959. As of this writing, it is still in print.

In present-day Japan, harmony still takes precedence over reality, but it is weaker than before and is very slowly giving away to the give-and-take kind of interaction that is favored by Americans and other Westerners. However, it is still considered a serious breach of etiquette to take a blunt, hard approach to any subject at the onset of any conversation.

As in virtually all other areas of typical Japanese behavior the role and importance of harmony was, and still is, an outgrowth of the emotional content in the Japanese mindset. The average Japanese simply cannot avoid reacting to things emotionally and read-ing a great deal more into situations than the situations often require or deserve.

There are exceptions, of course, among Japanese who have had substantial experience in interacting with Westerners, especially if they are able to communicate in English or any other non-Japanese language. But these exceptions may be little more than skin deep and still not reflect reality.

Since the early 1990s a growing number of Japanese who have become bilingual and at least partially bicultural have been haranguing their fellow countrymen to break out of this linguistic-based box in other to communicate more clearly and completely with others.

The Japanese are acutely aware of this factor in their relationships with others, but it is a cultural mold that is very difficult to break, and will no doubt continue to be characteristic of their behavior for some time.

The challenge for the Japanese is to develop the diplomatic skills that will make it possible for them to dispense with *tatemae* altogether, and communicate only their *honne*.

[XV]
Passivity vs. Aggressiveness

ANOTHER of the dichotomies in the Japanese character that is greatly influenced by their dual-brain orientation has to do with passivity and aggression. For centuries Japanese who were not members of the ruling samurai class were conditioned by their culture, and compelled by their system of government, to behave in an extraordinarily passive manner.

This passivity was based on precise forms of behavior toward everyone, but especially toward superiors and those with any kind of official authority. The sanctions enforcing this passivity were powerful and generally unforgiving. Two of the measures that were constantly over the heads of the common people like a sword were immediate death at the hands of a samurai warrior, and being ostracized by their group.

This conditioning in passivity during the long reign of the Shoguns (1192-1868) was so comprehensive that it became second nature to the common people—and gave early visitors to Japan the impression that ordinary Japanese were among the most peaceful and polite people on the planet.

And generally speaking this was true. By the same token, however, the Japanese were so susceptible to being controlled and molded by those in authority that they could be turned from their peaceful ways to acts of extreme violence in a very short period of time, as was starkly demonstrated by their wartime activities in the first half of the 20th century.

Still today, under normal circumstances, the Japanese are far more passive-minded than most Westerners, and they continue to accept regimentation more readily than others.

Individual aggression, especially in public, is still rare in Japan, although this too is increasing as the power of the traditional culture weakens. When aggressive behavior does occur it can be explosive because once the cultural restraints on such behavior are removed by some official edict, or thrown off in a personal action, the results can be extreme.

Emotional outbursts that lead to violence have also become more common in Japan, including in the Diet. These actions are caused by the fact that the Japanese have had little experience in the kind of hard-ball but non-violent debating that takes place between individuals and in government halls in the U.S., England and Europe.

Such give-and-take behavior is precisely the kind of exchanges that was taboo in traditional Japan, because it contradicted the imperative of harmony.

Because harmony traditionally took priority over the expression of emotion in Japan, the Japanese lived in a pressure cooker for generations; very calm on the surface but often seething with unfulfilled needs and unresolved anger.

The lid of this cultural pressure cooker was first unbolted in 1945 by the abolition of the feudalist family system and the removal of social, political and economic sanctions on independent thinking and behaving.

This gift of freedom did not immediately change the attitudes or behavior of most adult Japanese, especially the men. The conditioning they had been subjected to throughout their lives was too strong. Young women were the first to take advantage of this new freedom—since women are always more flexible and more practical than men.

The first generation of Japanese to escape much of the cultural conditioning that was responsible for the passive mindset of their parents and ancestors were those born after 1960, and it was this generation that began to weaken the molds of the past.

And yet again, the power of the traditional culture and the language is such that most Japanese still today live partially or totally in the cultural molds of the past. The lid is still on the cooker, and most Japanese must conform, emotionally and intellectually, to the dictates of their culture.

The challenge today is for the Japanese to try to achieve a better balance between the emotional side of their character and the objective, logical input from the left side of their brains.

[XVI]
Spirit vs. Reality

ANOTHER of the primary elements of the Japanese character heavily influenced by their dual left-brain orientation and its reservoir of emotions is their spirit—that is their will, their motivation, the power that drives them.

Very early in their history the Japanese became endowed with a spirit that they regarded as one of their most distinguishing and valuable characteristics. This spirit was called *Yamato damashii* (Yah-mah-toh dah-mah-she-ee), or "Japanese spirit," and was seen as the primary essence of the Japanese character and the foundation of their national identity.

The phrase first came into use over a thousand years ago to distinguish between native ideas, and patterns of thought imported from China. [Yamato was the original name the Japanese gave to their country, apparently taken from the name of the clan that founded the Imperial line.]

Later, the phrase was used in literary works and in military treatises to describe spiritual qualities that were supposedly unique to the Japanese, and included such attributes as devotion to country, sincerity, courage, strength of mind and the ability to endure pain and adversity.

Following the fall of the Shogunate form of government in 1867/8 the *Yamato damashii* concept was made the foundation of the training and indoctrination of the country's new Western style military forces. It was also made the cornerstone of the public school system.

This was the spirit that the new government invoked when it began a crash program to catch up with the West industrially and militarily. It was also the spirit that was called upon to inspire Japan's military forces during World War II, especially after it became obvious that the country was going to be defeated for the first time in its history.

Prior to World War II the Japanese were totally programmed in the idea that spirit would bring them victory over a much larger and more powerful adversary. They therefore fought with incredible tenacity and courage, and having lost the war turned this same spirit into rebuilding Japan and transforming their country into the world's second largest economy.

The spirit of the Japanese is still strong and still provides them with the will and energy that is reflected not only in their economic prowess, but also in the efficiency with which they operate their economy. It is the source of their drive for quality in everything they do.

[XVII]
Quality vs. Profit

ONE of the most extraordinary differences in the traditional culture of Japan and the post-industrialization cultures of the United States and Europe was that in Japan profit-making was regarded as immoral, while in these Western countries making a profit was the primary goal of all privately owned enterprises.

In the context of Japan's traditional culture, profit making was counter to the teachings of Buddhism and to the Japanese concept of humanism. In the Japanese view, the fundamental purpose of an enterprise was to provide an essential service to society.

Two of the most outstanding figures who followed this pattern were Sazo Idemitsu who established the forerunner of Idemitsu Oil Company in 1911, and Konosuke Matsushita, who in 1918 founded the tiny enterprise that was to become the giant Matsushita Electric Industrial Company.

Both Idemitsu and Matsushita preached and practiced the policy of living humble lives and managing their companies to provide the best possible products to society at an affordable price. Even though they had to make a profit, profits came after product quality and service to the public. Their philosophy was that if they made the best products that could be made and served the public with absolute sincerity and diligence, the public would buy from them and they would make a profit.

It is still accurate to say that among the vast majority of Japanese companies, quality and service are regarded as important as profits. And while the origin of this philosophy can no doubt be traced to the influence of Buddhism, the overall humanistic values of the Japanese grew out of the left-brain centered emotional elements in their culture.

Japanese companies must now compete on price with foreign firms that generally adjust their quality standards to squeeze as much profit as possible out of their products. This is making it increasingly difficult for the Japanese to maintain their standards.

So far they have managed to compete on the basis of both quality and price by utilizing superior manufacturing and testing procedures and virtually eliminating defective products. But there may be a limit to how long they can depend upon this approach, as a growing number of American and other firms have adopted—and sometimes improved on—the Japanese techniques of manufacturing and quality control.

If Japanese companies can hang onto the philosophy that quality and service are on the same plane as profit, they will be among those that deserve to survive into the future.

[XVIII]
Diligence vs. Getting By

UNTIL around 1980, one of the cultural factors that gave Japanese companies an advantage over foreign companies was the fact that Japanese workers, as a rule, were significantly more diligent in their efforts than their foreign counterparts.

There were exceptions on the foreign side, or course, but they were exceptions, not the rule, and this made a fundamental difference in the productivity and competitive power of individual companies.

However, by the late 1990s the famous diligence of Japanese workers had begun to erode around the edges, and that of American and other workers had improved—primarily because of real and perceived competition from Japan.

Still, on a one-to-one basis the typical Japanese worker is generally more diligent than his or her foreign counterpart, whose philosophy more often than not is to do just enough to get by.

The Japanese owe their traditional diligence to Zen Buddhism, to the master-apprentice approach to learning, and to a code of ethics that did not tolerate insincere and inefficient behavior, or shoddy work.

There was another cultural factor in the diligence of the Japanese that was of equal importance. And that was shame. Striving to achieve perfection in everything they did raised normal expectations to a very high level in Japanese society.

Not being totally diligent in their efforts—regardless of the outcome—was considered shameful and un-Japanese, and that was something the Japanese could not stand. They were exceedingly sensitive to shame and any sign of disrespect, and were thus motivated to extend themselves in whatever they did.

In this social environment, unstinting effort was the key to approval and respect, and was praised and honored.

Here again, this mindset primarily derived from the emotional content of the Japanese character. Rather than taking an objective, rational approach to quitting when things got hard, and when they appeared to be impossible, the Japanese were prompted by their feelings to redouble their efforts.

This trait has long been visible in Japanese behavior, going back to the days of the samurai, to their military endeavors in more recent times, and finally in their extraordinary feat of not only rebuilding Japan after World War II but transforming the country into an economic superpower in just two and a half decades.

In fact, diligence was one of the primary lessons taught directly and indirectly by Japan's traditional culture—in the home, in school, in sports, and in work. It was so much a part of the culture that it was taken for granted.*

---

*It is recorded that in the 1930s students striving to memorize English words in dictionaries would study them, then tear the pages out and eat them to physically absorb the meanings.

By the end of the 20th century, much of the indoctrination of diligence by both parents and schools had diminished significantly, resulting in the first generation of Japanese in which there were large numbers of individuals who were less motivated and less diligent than those who came before them.

While the influence of the Japanese language on this new generation remains essentially the same, the emotional content of their character is no longer channeled into behavior marked by diligence. The number of Japanese who are far less diligent than older generations is growing exponentially.

If this trend continues—and it surely will—it will have a profoundly negative influence on the future of Japan.

As for the "just enough to get by" trend that began to afflict American workers in the 1950s, the downward movement appears to have slowed dramatically, and from around 1975 began inching upward—again, primarily because of competition from Japan, which at that time seemed destined to economically colonize the world.

If Japan is to retain its position as an economic superpower, it must once again make the concept and practice of diligence a primary part of the Japanese character.

[XIX]
Risk-Aversion vs. Risk-Taking

WITH the exception of ill-founded military ventures that ended in 1945, the Japanese have traditionally been adverse to risk-taking, not only as a national group, but down to the attitudes and behavior of individuals.

The traditional risk-aversion mindset of the Japanese did not derive primarily from their brain orienttation—which one might assume would have made them more likely to take risks because they were driven more by emotion and an exaggerated spirit than by rational thinking.

In fact, it was this emotion-charged spirit that led Japanese leaders to engage in military adventures that ended in Japan's defeat in World War II, and brought home to the Japanese the folly of spirit-driven risk-taking.

The traditional Japanese aversion to risk-taking came from cultural factors that had very little to do the dominance of the left side of their brains—although this factor made their aversion to risking-taking stronger.

Their aversion to risk-taking developed in ancient times because their social and political systems made it both immoral and dangerous. In harmony-conscious Japan, anything that might result in disharmony was taboo. Risk-taking on any level can be disruptive when it fails, it was therefore bad.

As time passed, this aversion to taking risks permeated the mindset of the people, and was further buttressed by the prevailing philosophy of group-orientation and decision-making by consensus—both of which were designed to reduce the danger of risk-taking by making such actions difficult to carry out, and mitigating personal responsibility when something did go wrong.

The influence of these cultural factors is still very obvious in present-day Japan. Risk-taking is still looked upon as immoral to some extent and as a last resort when there is no other choice.

This factor is a primary element in the tendency for Japanese companies to form consortiums and groups when undertaking ventures that require some risk, and to deal only with Japanese companies when they have a choice.

However, by the beginning of the 21st century the aversion to risk that had been built into Japan's culture had become a major handicap, not only internationally but domestically as well. Consultants, educators and others had begun to preach that the Japanese had to discard the old way of thinking and behaving, and begin taking risks.

The older and larger the Japanese company, the more difficult it is for it to change its ways. The older individual managers and executives, the more likely they are to fear and shy away from risk-taking. But they are acutely aware of the need for a new mindset.

Many of these companies have established wholly-owed subsidiaries that are staffed with young employees who have been given the authority to take risks because there is simply no other way for them to gain the advantage of carefully planned gambling on a new product or service.

Despite substantial progress in suppressing the age-old cultural taboos against risk-taking and the left-brain fears of failure, the combination of these two factors continue to influence the Japanese and must be dealt with in dealing with them.

On the plus side, the Japanese are now much more willing to accept foreigner investors and partners, and to follow through on their famous *kyosei* (k'yoh-say-ee) concept of global economic integration.

[XX]
Sincerity vs. Insincerity

THE Japanese have traditionally regarded themselves as among the most sincere people on the planet—a belief that grew out of their commitment to harmony, which incorporated a cooperative attitude, humility, honesty, veracity, respect and goodwill—all Japanese style, of course.

While this commitment to harmony was reinforced by their right-brain qualities of spirituality, attunement with nature and humanistic feelings, the core of their sincerity evolved out of the obligations they owed to the social and political systems under which they lived, particularly following the beginning of rule by the samurai class in 1192.

The warrior-administered government simply imposed a system of laws on the people that were designed to ensure harmony, and then enforced the laws with stern measures that guaranteed they would be obeyed.

Over the centuries, the Japanese were thus mentally and physically programmed to behave in a precise manner that came to be equated with sincerity in all things—a type of behavior that would ensure harmony in all human relationships.

In essence, this meant that the Japanese would not do anything that would result in friction or disharmony, which typically meant suppressing their emotions, doing things they did not want to do, and being tolerant of the behavior of others in the expectation of receiving similar treatment in the future.

In short, the Japanese definition of sincerity is doing whatever is necessary to create and sustain harmony in all relationships. Insincerity is any attitude or behavior that disrupts the harmony of the group or the enterprise.

In the past, there was also a tendency for the Japanese to regard the Western custom of resorting to hard facts and logic in decision-making as a form of insincerity, because such behavior frequently ignored human feelings and individual needs, which in traditional Japanese values had the highest priority.

Although weakened by shifts in cultural values, this cultural concept is still very much alive in the mindset of the Japanese, and is still discernible in their day-to-day behavior in business as well as in social relationships—a factor foreign businesspeople find disconcerting if they are not aware of why it exists and how it works.

[XXI]
Wet vs. Dry

WHEN the Japanese first began to encounter Westerners in the 1500s they quickly became aware that there were fundamental differences in their attitudes and behavior regarding virtually every thing, from bathing (which the Japanese did daily and the Westerners hardly every did) and food to sex—not to mention the conduct of business and personal relationships.

Many of the individualistic attitudes and practices of the Westerners were emotionally and intellectually shocking to the Japanese, whose etiquette and lifestyle were highly organized according to precise patterns of behavior that went back centuries.

However, these differences did not have any tangible affect on the vast majority of the Japanese at that time, because they never as much as seen Westerners, much less interacted with them in any way.

It was not until the 1850s and beyond that relatively small numbers of Japanese in main cities like Edo (Tokyo) began to occasionally see Westerners. By the late 1800s there were several thousand Westerners in Japan, but still most Japanese never saw any of them.

In fact, it was not until the fall of 1945 and the following years, during which there were several hundred thousand Westerners in Japan—including some of the more remote areas of the country—that Japanese and Westerners began to interact in large numbers, both officially and unofficially.

This interaction between hundreds of thousand of Japanese and Westerners took place on every level of society, from the top of the political heap and the business elite, down to employees in shops, bars, inns, restaurants and other facilities.

It was the almost immediate unofficial interaction between Japanese women and Westerner men that was to have the fastest, most conspicuous and most fundamental impact on the culture of the country. Less than a year after the arrival of Western Occupation forces in Japan, daily liaisons between the troops and young women numbered in the hundreds of thousands.

The cultural changes that were to remake Japan over the next decades began among the ranks of these young women, many of them employed by the Occupation forces and the others serving in other capacities.

The economic contributions the free-spending GI's made to Japan's war-devastated economy amounted to millions of dollars a month. The volume of American goods diverted into the black-market, often from GI's through their Japanese girl friends, was astounding.

By the early 1950s popular interest magazines had begun to cover the hundreds of thousands of foreign-Japanese liaisons that had been formed, and to highlight the cultural the differences of the people involved. One especially astute writer began referring to the Japanese as "wet" and to Westerners as "dry,"—a phraseology I believe originated with another Japanese writer in the 1920s.

In its Japanese context, a "wet" person is one who gives precedence to emotions and feelings—in other words, an emotion-driven Japanese. A "dry" person is one who automatically applies logic and reason to every situation he or she confronts, whether it is business or a private matter—in other words, a left-brained foreigner.

The 1950s writer went on to provide warnings for the thousands of young Japanese women who were intimately involved with foreign men. Some of his warnings were that foreign men were too objective, too unfeeling, to be suitable for Japanese women, and that foreign men would use them and then leave them.

In an ironic twist, young Japanese women today often criticize Japanese men for being too dry—uncaring and cold—while the image of foreign men has been more or less reversed, and they are now seen as wetter than their Japanese counterparts.

As soon as the Occupation authorities allowed Western businessmen to enter Japan in the late 1940s they, too, began to encounter the dry-wet phenomenon, although it was not referred to in this terminology.

In addition to the basic communications problem resulting from the fact that the Western businesspeople invariably did not speak Japanese—and it was left up to the Japanese to overcome the language barrier—both sides suffered from clashes between their wet and dry natures.

Since that long ago time, Japanese businesspeople have become dryer. Significant numbers of them can communicate in English or other Western languages, and they have had more than a generation of experience dealing with left-brain people.

For their part, most Western businesspeople dealing with the Japanese are now far more culturally sensitive and knowledgeable. Thousands of them have spent years in Japan and many now speak the language well.

All these things combined have taken much of the friction and pain out of Japanese-foreign business relationships. But the basic differences between wet and dry people are such that problems still arise, and it requires special effort to build and sustain harmonious relationships.

As with most of Japan's other cultural traits that evolved from their dual left-brain orientation, their "wet" characteristics are in tune with the fundamental changes taking place in all societies worldwide—meaning that the humanistic approach to life is gradually coming into its own.

One of the ways the Japanese measure their humanistic view of relationships [outside of the context of enemies!] is in "Emotional Intelligence"—meaning the degree of influence positive emotions have on individuals. The stronger this influence the higher the E.I. and the more *Japanese* the behavior.

[XXII]
Dual-Brain Views That Distinguish the Japanese

Aesthetics
The Japanese view and use of aesthetics is one of the most conspicuous characteristics that distinguish them,

at least to some extent, from virtually all other people on the planet—a factor that helps to corroborate Dr. Tadano Tsunoda's theory that the emotional side of the Japanese is housed in the left side of their brains and is therefore influenced by rational thinking.

One might say, in fact, that the whole of Japan's traditional culture was based on aesthetics that were created and defined by a combination of logic and emotion.

There were no areas of Japan's traditional lifestyle that did not have a significant aesthetic element. Their arts, their crafts, their wearing apparel, their presentation of food, their stylized etiquette, all were infused with aesthetic elements. Even the ritual of *harakiri* (hah-rah-kee-ree), or suicide by slicing the stomach open, was performed with aesthetic style.

Obviously, left-brain oriented Westerners and other non-Japanese are fully capable of recognizing and appreciating beauty, but aesthetics is not a primary controlling factor in the thinking and behavior of most of them and plays only a minor role in their daily lives.

This is especially true of left-brain oriented non-Japanese men, with the general exceptions being those whose female side is strong enough to influence their attitudes and behavior. Of course, left-brained men who are homosexual are primarily motivated by feminine instincts, which accounts for their emphasis on feelings and their refined tastes.

The dual-brained based aesthetic foundation of Japanese culture has proven to be one of their most valuable assets in virtually every field of endeavor, providing elements of beauty, harmony, and sophistication that are pleasing to the body, the mind and the soul.

The Japanese traditionally came by their aesthetic asset naturally because it was built into the culture. But they did not stop there. They devised a variety of practices that were designed specifically to exercise and expand their aesthetic abilities.

While only a small percentage of the Japanese today actively engage in aesthetic practices on a regular basis, all continue to be influenced by the ongoing aesthetic content of the culture. And Japan as a whole continues to benefit from this remarkable advantage.

Apparel

There are two historical factors in the Japanese view and reaction to wearing apparel. One of them is a result of the influence of their dual-brain orientation. The other is the fact that during the last Shogunate regime (1603-1868), the clothing that people could wear was determined by the government, and was based on their social class and occupation.

Government control of the apparel that the Japanese were allowed to wear during the Tokugawa Shogunate era made them extraordinarily sensitive to clothing because it designated one's legal and hereditary social class. Wearing clothing that was not approved for one's class was against the law.

The laws regarding wearing apparel were so detailed that they included the precise date in the spring when the population was required to change from winter to summer clothing, and again in the fall when the whole country changed back to winter clothing.

By the latter decades of the 17th century, members of the merchant class who had become affluent began to circumvent this law by wearing expensive and colorful underclothing beneath their drab outer robes.

Laws controlling what the Japanese could wear disappeared in 1868 when the Tokugawa Shogunate was abolished, although some urban Japanese had been ignoring the laws with impunity for several years.

With the influx of Western technology and Western ideas from 1870 on, urban Japanese also began gradually switching over to Western style clothing. One of the factors that played a key role in this changeover was the appearance of streetcars and trains. It was difficult, and sometimes virtually impossible, for people wearing tight-fitting kimono to step up into these new forms of transportation with their dignity intact.

It was not until the years following the end of World War II in 1945 that virtually all Japanese made the switch to the more practical Western style clothing. The kimono remained the formal dress of both men and women, but it was generally worn only on special occasions, such as weddings and official ceremonies.

However, the traditional thin kimono-like cotton *yukata* (yuu-kah-tah) robe continued to be worn around the house as casual wear and as a bathrobe, as well as the apparel of choice during participation in festivals and at hot spring spas.

The yukata continues to be a common item in the Japanese wardrobe (and is provided to guests by virtually all inns and hotels).

The strong emotional element in the character of the Japanese made their perspective of clothing primarily feminine—that is, primarily based on feelings, which resulted in them being exceptionally sensitive about the fabric, the color, the design and the finish of the clothing.

This special sensitivity to clothing is still very strong in present-day Japan, and is most obvious in the traditional kimono, in which the imperative for harmony and compatibility include both the gender and the age of the individual wearer.

Ready-made clothing in Japan today is, of course, overwhelmingly Western in style and reflects the sensibilities of Westerners, but the emotional and feminine character of the Japanese makes them conspicuously more style and quality conscious than the typical Westerner.

Art

Most of Japan's art traditions were introduced into the country by Chinese and Korean immigrants between 300 and 700 A.D., and most were a part of the paraphernalia of Buddhism.

But over the following centuries these arts and crafts became Japanized as a result of a unique mind-set that continues to distinguish the Japanese today.

As already noted, a significant facet of the unique mentality of the Japanese is a result of their emotional responses coming from the left side of their brains where they are influenced by logical, rational thought.

The combined influence of the emotional and rational elements in Japanese thinking has given their traditional arts an aesthetic and philosophical quality that reflects their distinctive sensibilities.

Traditional Japanese art generally consists of a dream-like view of nature with the details only suggested, leaving it up to the viewer to fill in the image from his or her own experience and view of nature.

In those arts and crafts where there is more detail, the subjects are imbued with a humanistic touch that brings out the spirituality of the subject. Harmony, tranquility and a sense of soulful repose are hallmarks of Japanese art.

Beauty
The Japanese are, I believe, the only people whose traditional culture included the recognition and appreciation of beauty as one of its primary elements and who have succeeded in surviving, along with the beauty-based aspects of their culture, into modern times.

It appears that the impulse that was responsible for the Japanese attachment to beauty grew out of Shinto, the indigenous religion of the Japanese, which was essentially nature worship and which was dramatically influenced by the extraordinary beauty of the Japanese islands.

In any event, the Japanese concept of beauty grew out of nature. That which was natural was beautiful and was to be respected and emulated. Customs and rituals to commune with the beauty of nature, and with man-made objects that emulated nature, became an integral part of the life of the people.

With nature as the standard of beauty by which all things were judged, the Japanese went on to develop vocabulary that expressed specific qualities of beauty, making it possible to describe and discuss them.

One of the key words in this vocabulary was *shibui* (she-booey), which, in its aesthetic sense, means simple and refined; with all extraneous parts eliminated, leaving the essence of the object revealed. Another key aesthetic term was *yugen* (yuu-gane), meaning "mystery" or "sub-tlety," referring to a type of beauty that lies beneath the surface of the material but is in delicate harmony with it, and registers on both the conscious and subconscious mind of the viewer. *Yugen* radiates a kind of spiritual essence.

A third term in the aesthetic vocabulary of the Japanese is *myo* (m'yoh), which by itself means strangeness or mystery, combined with skill. Japan's famed Zen master Daisetsu Suzuki said that *myo* is the expression of a quality that transcends the skill of the artist or craftsman, and is a reflection of the cosmic spirit that is inherent in things.

Suzuki added that the reason why so few Westerners are able to "see" the *myo* of art and craft objects is that their concept of beauty is based on conscious realization, with the result that their ego prevents them from seeing beyond the mechanical skill of the maker. He also says that it is the *myo* of Japanese arts and crafts that give them the distinctive, unique aura that makes them "Japanese."

It seems that by the beginning of the 21st century commercial designers in the United States had, in fact, begun to transcend their own cultural conditioning and their egos to produce designs that do, in fact, reflect *myo*—again primarily as a result of both competition and insight gained from dual-brain created Japanese designs.

Bathing

Historically, one of the weirdest aberrations of Christianity and other religions was associating bathing with undesirable if not sinful sexual behavior, and avoiding it (bathing, not sex) altogether except on rare occasions.

One of the first things Western missionaries did when they arrived in Japan in the mid-1500s, and again in the last half of the 1800s, was to prohibit their converts from bathing every day—a practice that had been an integral part of Japanese culture since ancient times. When the missionaries finally realized how traumatic this ban was, they relented to the point of allowing Japanese Christians to bathe a few times a month.

Obviously, the Christian missionaries had no idea whatsoever of the spiritual importance of daily bathing to the Japanese. Shinto, the indigenous religion of the Japanese, taught that there were two forms of cleanliness—physical and spiritual—and that bathing daily cleansed both the body and the spirit.

The concept of spiritual cleansing with water was not unknown in the West. It was, in fact, common in Roman culture and in other ancient societies. It did not become stigmatized for the majority of mankind until the appearance of Christianity and Islam.

But the Christian church did not wholly abandon the ancient connection between water and spiritual cleansing. It was kept as an integral part of the baptismal ceremony by sprinkling water on babies or dunking adults in rivers or lakes.

The typical Westerner of today automatically associates bathing with getting rid of grime, sweat and body order—a strictly left-brain action—even though there is some awareness that a deep, warm or hot bath soothes the spirit as well as the body, and is often far more effective than praying in restoring the soul to equilibrium.

I recommend that Western cultures switch their left-brain concept of bathing to the right-brain, and reap both the physical and spiritual benefits that are provided by water.

Business Management

All of the aspects of Japan's traditional way of managing that are different from the Western way—and responsible for most of the problems that develop between the Japanese and non-Japanese in business, in education, in politics and in all other affairs involving human interaction—are a direct result of the emotional orientation of the Japanese and the logical orientation of non-Japanese.

In the simplest terms, these differences and problems arise because non-Japanese tend to base their attitudes and behavior on linear thinking and reasoning, while the Japanese tend to think and behave in holistic and human terms.

There is an emotional element in every custom, every practice, that defines the characteristic Japanese way of doing things. In contrast, the prevailing Western way of managing since beginning of the Industrial Age was to reduce or eliminate altogether the emotional element in their management.

In some cases, the differences that arise from emotion-drive and logic-driven approaches are minor and can often be resolved fairly easily. In other cases, the two sides are simply too far apart to reach a compromise.

For their part, many of the Japanese involved in dealing with non-Japanese have become skilled to varying degrees in using the logic software in the left side of their brains, particularly if they are using a foreign language. Hang-ups still occur among this group, however, because they are often not the final decision-makers in their companies, and still have to work in harmony with company members.

Native left-brain thinkers engaging in business and other affairs with the Japanese are generally less skilled in taking emotion-based positions and less inclined to do so when problems arise. Their normal reaction, usually automatic, is that their position is rational, reasonable and fair so altering it doesn't make sense.

Of course, the basic Japanese reaction is that their position is also the right one, and they rationalize and compromise their position only when they perceive that not doing so would result in a greater disadvantage.

Given the various circumstances of Japan's position in relation to the rest of the world, the Japanese are more likely than non-Japanese to make compromises in order to create and sustain relationships.

Interestingly, there have been numerous situations in the past where the non-Japanese side held fast to their positions in the face of Japanese opposition, only to discover later that they would have been significantly better off if they had accepted the Japanese position.

When dealing with the Japanese, non-Japanese are advised to put their right-brain caps on and evaluate the situation from that side of their head before coming to final conclusions.

Bragging

Bragging—which is especially characteristic of Americans—may seem to a left-brain person to be of small consequence, but it goes against the cultural grain of the Japanese (and many other people), and is seen as both arrogant and uncultured, if not immoral.

The primary thrust of Japan's traditional culture was harmony first and last, and any kind of behavior that upset this harmony was seen as undesirable. Instead of bragging about their accomplishments or skills, it was characteristic of the Japanese to conceal them to avoid appearing conceited or arrogant—and to be able to suddenly use them to catch people off guard and gain an advantage, or to surprise them and win their praise.

Bragging is still taboo as far as most Japanese are concerned, but there are growing numbers who are breaking this cultural mold because of new found courage and individuality—both of which are now approved of, in principle, by businesspeople, politicians and some bureaucrats.

Of course, the people in this latter category are generally the young and those who have been partially or completely de-Japanized by long-term exposure to Western, especially American, influences.

When contemplated by the left side of the brain, bragging is often a rational and reasonable thing to do, especially when the individual concerned can back up his or her claims by producing or excelling in some way. It becomes immoral if it is intended to deceive.

Whether or not left-brain people should brag to the Japanese is therefore a moral judgment. The same rules should apply to the Japanese. Just as overstating "facts" is immoral, concealing facts in order to gain an unfair advantage is also immoral.

One of the advantages that accrue to the Japanese as a result of the cultural taboo against bragging is that they are often underestimated and not taken seriously, resulting in competitors and opponents lowering their guard and becoming more susceptible to being beaten.

Cuteness
One of the more conspicuous elements in Japanese culture is what amounts to a virtual obsession with cuteness—individuals and things that are delightfully pretty and dainty. This compulsive attachment to cuteness especially applies to young girls, to small animals and to small objects, and is manifested widely in the culture, in toys, other products, printed advertisements, television commercials, cartoons and comics.

In the past, Westerners were inclined to view the attachment of adult Japanese to cuteness as a weakness, regarding it as immature, if not infantile. This foreign attitude tended to lead Westerners to underestimate the intellectual and physical abilities of the Japanese.

The accomplishments of the Japanese in the interim have pretty much eliminated this Western attitude, and now the Japanese penchant for building cuteness into things is being emulated in the West.

As it happened, there is a deep-seated part of the Western psyche that remembers the cuteness of infants and other small things, and now, with the success of the Japanese in merchandising cuteness so obvious, Westerners are not only allowing these emotions to surface, they are consciously making use of them.

So here, again, we have the emotional orientation of the Japanese turning out to be a significant advantage in both product design and marketing.

Decision-Making
Western businesspeople and diplomats who have encountered the Japanese way of making decisions might have some difficulty relating the process to positive aspects of their dual-brain orientation, but a very good case can be made.

Two of the most common complaints that Westerners have traditionally lodged against their Japanese counterparts is the length of time it takes the Japanese to make decisions, and the fact that once they are made the Japanese do not necessarily treat them as complete, as done.

The reason it takes the Japanese time to make most decisions is simple: they are made by consensus among many people, not by single individuals. By using the consensus approach to decisions the Japanese are more likely to have the full support of everyone involved in whatever commitment is made.

There is an old saying that American businesspeople make decisions in a matter of hours if not minutes and then need a year or so to implement them, while the Japanese may take a year to make a decision but once the decision is made they implement it immediately.

The Japanese approach to decision-making incorporates the feelings and factual input from anywhere to a few to dozens of individuals, contributing to both the quality of the decision and the chances that it will be carried out successfully.

This holistic approach to contemplating new ideas, new relationships, and decision-making has proven to be a major advantage for the Japanese. Just one example: from day one, the Japanese routinely involve product designers, engineers and assembly line experts in the process of creating new products, thereby avoiding many of the production and quality problems that so often plague American manufacturers.

And this is another example of Japan's human-oriented right-brain/left-brain ingenuity that has since been copied by Westerners, particularly American car manufacturers.

Etiquette
The Japanese have been famous for centuries for their highly stylized and ritualized system of etiquette. The dual-brain orientation of the Japanese was certainly not exclusively responsible for the creation of this eti-

quette, but it had a great deal to do with its creation and its survival since ancient times.

The earliest day-to-day behavior of the Japanese was influenced by Shinto, which incorporated paying highly formalized respect to the numerous gods that made up the Japanese pantheon. From the 6th through the 7th centuries, Japanese behavior was further influenced by the etiquette of Imperial China, with its respect forms of stylized behavior, titles and wearing apparel.

Next came Japan's samurai class of warriors who ruled the country from 1192 until 1868. The code of ethics and etiquette that the samurai developed during this long reign—particularly from 1603 on—infused the culture of Japan with a form of etiquette that was as precise, as detailed, as the behavior of actors on a stage.

Westerners who encountered Japanese in the early 1600s and again in the late 1800s were so impressed with the behavior of the average person they equated it with what one might expect of members of a royal court.

The traditional etiquette of the Japanese thus became a major asset that gave them a significant advantage in dealing with non-Japanese, especially Westerners whose manners were generally crude by comparison.

Still today, Westerners in Japan are generally intimidated by the style and formality of Japanese etiquette, and generally go further than they normally do to avoid offending anyone. In this effort, it is common for Westerners to become less critical and more accommodating in their interactions with the Japanese, providing the Japanese with an advantage.

Flattery
In a society in which blunt comments and direct criticism were traditionally taboo, and could get one shortened by a head, the custom of flattery not only became universal, it was developed into a fine art. Flattery thus became one of the tools (or weapons!) that the Japanese consistently used in their dealings with others.

When the Japanese first began encountering Westerners it did not take them long to discover that the foreigners were especially susceptible to effusive praise, and that most of them could be manipulated like puppets.

The Japanese were, and still are, especially clever in the use of flattery because their dual-brain orienttation has made them extraordinarily experienced in dealing with, and playing on, human emotions.

Humility
The Japanese have always been among the proudest people on earth—at least in part because their creation myth says they were not just created by gods, but that they were the direct progeny of gods. [That's a lot more impressive than being made out of dirt and then infused with life!]

In any event, unbounded pride has been one of the primary characteristics of the Japanese since ancient times, and has played a leading role in their history on an individual as well as a national basis.

This pride has manifested itself in a variety of ways, in virtually every facet of Japanese culture and accomplishment—from the incredible skill of the samurai in swordsmanship, the mastery of the arts and crafts, to today's success in the production of consumer and industrial goods.

What is remarkable about the pride of the Japanese, and what is quite different from the way of Americans and other Westerners, is that in Japanese culture individually expressing or behaving in a prideful manner was taboo and regarded as a serious offense.

Humility, the exact opposite of prideful behavior, was seen as one of the prime virtues, and the Japanese were conditioned to conduct themselves in a humble way, especially toward superiors.

Behaving in a humble manner is still characteristic of the Japanese, and commonly results in them gaining an advantage. Americans in particular appear to be psychologically programmed to go out of their way to help people who act in a humble manner.

Generally, Americans automatically equate humble behavior with lack of confidence, lack of experience, lack of ability, lack of knowledge, etc., and the tendency is for them to go out of their way to help such individuals.

The traditionally humble mode of the Japanese has probably got them more help from good-intentioned Americans and other Westerners than can be imagined—often without them asking for it. All they have to do to turn the typical American on is to act like they don't know what is going on.

Interestingly, the Japanese have the same psychological conditioning where non-Japanese are concerned. They ordinarily do not go out of their way to help other Japanese except in business situations because of the potential of incurring social responsibilities but like Americans, they have a compulsion to help foreigners—especially those who are short-term visitors.

Still, in business situations the Japanese generally get more from Americans than what they give because the average American does not behave in a humble manner, and typically does not give the impression of needing help. But all they have to do is ask. This immediately puts the average Japanese in the help mode.

Mentoring in all areas of life is traditional among older Japanese, and they are especially programmed to help younger people. The humanistic influence of their emotional orientation is responsible for this trait.

Intelligence
There are several kinds of intelligence, all generally recognized by people in all cultures. But the emphasis that cultures put on the different kinds of intelligence varies greatly. The Japanese have traditionally empha-

sized and developed their insight (intelligence) in human relations.

In effect, Japan's culture has traditionally given the highest priority to "emotional intelligence"—not book learning or the intelligence gained from practical experience. The cultural and social standing of people was generally measured in terms of their insight into human behavior and how to help themselves and others keep their emotions in balance.

Part of this emphasis came from the emotional content of their left-brain orientation. Another part came from the influence of Shinto and Buddhism, both of which emphasize physical, emotional and spiritual harmony.

Emotional intelligence continues to play a significant role in the Japanese penchant for working in groups, for resolving issues and making decisions by consensus, and for going out of their way to avoid disharmony.

Problems often arise, however, in their dealings with Westerners and others who do not give the same weight to emotional intelligence and in some cases ignore it altogether. The sensible recourse for the foreign side is, of course, to be aware on the role of emotional intelligence in Japanese life, and learn how to deal with it in an effective manner.

Mental Health
The cultural and social imperative of harmony in Japan's traditional society, which was both secular and

spiritual in nature, made the Japanese especially sensitive to attitudes, moods and one's overall mental health.

This sensitivity played a fundamental role in the day-to-day etiquette that distinguished Japanese behavior, as well as in the creation and role of customs or rituals that were designed to soothe the spirit, eliminate emotional turmoil, and satisfy the intellect.

The most famous of these rituals was the tea ceremony. Other mass customs included flower-viewing, snow-viewing, writing poetry and communing with nature through landscaped gardens, mountains and woodlands.

Another national custom that was unique to Japan, in the sense that it was institutionalized as a cultural practice, was the holding of year-end parties called *bonenkai* (boh-nane-kigh), or "forget the year parties."

What was specifically unique to the *bonenkai*, which are still common in present-day Japan, is that they are designed to help people rid themselves of any angry feelings that may have developed during the year against family members, co-workers and others.

This mass release of emotional grudges and hang-ups, a strictly right-brain function, contributes enormously to the mental health of the Japanese, and is a major factor in keeping the level of personal violence very low in society.

In other words, a combination of left-brain reasoning and right-brain wisdom resulted in the Japanese creating a cultural solution to psychological problems that are bound to arise among people—a factor that, until recent times, accounted for a very low incidence of psychiatric problems among the Japanese.

The rest of the world would be well-served by adopting and institutionalizing the Japanese custom of the *bonenkai*.

Problem Solving
The Japanese are especially good at solving esoteric and technical problems, as is evidenced by their rapid adaptation of Western technology and their own technological innovations and discoveries once the Tokugawa Shogunate ban on change and research disappeared in the 1860s. [Japanese scientists were close to having their own an atomic bomb when World War II ended.]

While there had been almost no basic scientific research in Japan prior to the latter decades of the 19th century, the Japanese had been exposed to the highly sophisticated technology of the arts and crafts of China since the 6th century, and over the generations had made significant improvements in many of the manufacturing processes they learned from China and Korea.

Earthquake technology, for example, was highly developed in Japan by the time of the construction of the great Todai Temple in Nara in 724-749. Modern day engineers who have been involved in maintenance on the building have been astounded by the construction techniques used to protect it from earthquakes. [It is said to be the largest wooden building in the world, and still today is an awesome sight.]

Throughout Japan's history the Japanese have not only been able to quickly understand any foreign technology that came their way, they have invariably been able to make improvements in it.

This impressive intellectual and technical ability of the early Japanese no doubt had its roots in a combination of factors, including, once again, the right-brain orientation that resulted in them looking at things from all angles, being able to visualize them in various three-dimensional forms, and predict their behavior in these new forms.

A second factor in the intellectual prowess of the Japanese had to have been Zen Buddhism, which taught them to focus with laser-like intensity, and to use what might be called a "third eye" to grasp the inner workings of things.

A third factor that surely contributed to the problem-solving ability of the Japanese is their historical custom of working together in teams, traditionally in groups of five. If two heads are better than one, five heads should be better than two. [Recent research has proven that the wisdom of groups generally adds up to more than the combination of individual intelligence.]

I believe that a fourth factor in the capacity of the Japanese to visualize intricate forms and recognize their relationship and coherency are the *Kanji* (Kahn-jee), the Chinese-created ideograms with which the Japanese write the core words of their language.

In early times, all educated Japanese learned how to read and draw at many as 5,000 of these ideograms, a process that trained the eye, the mind, and the hand to see small intricate forms clearly and to duplicate them with considerable skill.

Present-day Japanese students are required to learn only 1,945 Kanji, and many of them soon forget some of the more complicated and less used ideograms after they leave school. But learning even this comparatively small number of ideograms has a discernible, positive influence on the mindset and manual skills of the Japanese.

Self-Respect & Pride
One of the traditional characteristics of the Japanese was an extraordinarily strong sense of self-respect as individuals, as members of certain groups, and as Japanese

The exceptional sense of self-respect that distinguished the Japanese evolved out of the very high standards of behavior set by their culture and the social system under which they had lived since ancient times.

Self-respect could only be earned by successfully conforming to all of the demands of the culture and social system. In other words, Japanese style self-respect was not based on individual knowledge, skills, accomplishments or feelings of self-worth. It was based on behaving in the prescribed and expected manner.

The social system required the Japanese to think and behave as members of groups. With few if any exceptions, behaving as individuals on the basis of self-interest was regarded as anti-social and anti-Japanese. Even self-employed artists and craftsmen had to conform to a variety of customs and rules to avoid being ostracized.

Likewise, the extraordinary pride of the Japanese was not an individualized thing. It was based on the shared culture and on all of the accomplishments of the past—on the Japanese concept of themselves as members of an extraordinary race, as the creators of an extraordinary culture, and as a people with a spirit that set them apart from all others.

While events in modern times have dramatically changed the Japanese view of themselves, making them far less ethnocentric, they continue to be motivated by a strong sense of self-respect and pride that is reflected in their economic success and in their growing role in international affairs—all fueled by contributions from their unique brain orientation.

Sex

One of the most important factors in Japan's traditional culture came from the very core of Shintoism—which is essentially nature worship based on fertility.

Many of the Shinto gods of Japan (there were eight million of them!) were specifically concerned with fertility, which, in human terms, means sex. But rather than repress the sexual impulse and make it a sin—as the earthly representatives of some foreign gods did—Japan's gods celebrated sex

The Japanese were generally wise enough to recognize that people need to engage in sex regularly in order to remain physically, emotionally and spiritually healthy. They were thus spared the mental agony and physical suffering that has been inflicted on Jews, Christians and Muslims as a result of their irrational and inhuman denial and repression of the sexual impulse.

It may be a stretch to some to say that one of the reasons the Japanese are a successful people is because they did not turn sex into a sin and make it one of the most destructive forces ever unleashed on humanity.

In any event, I believe the fact that Japan avoided being Christianized and Westernized in earlier times contributed immeasurably to its subsequent economic success.*

---

*For a definitive explanation of the traits that have made the Japanese so successful economically, see the author's *THE JAPANESE SAMURAI CODE—Classic Strategies for Success* (Tuttle Publishing). It is available from online booksellers and bookstores.

Shame

As mentioned earlier, the emotional/logical orientation of the Japanese led them to be extraordinarily conscious of and sensitive to the behavior of others, resulting in them developing a "shame culture" rather than the kind of "guilt culture" that is characteristic of Christian, Jewish and Islamic societies.

Japanese behavior has never been controlled by internal feelings of guilt and fear of punishment by some unseen, all-powerful god. Their behavior has been controlled by feelings of shame that resulted if they did not conform to precise standards of etiquette and behavior that were visible for all to see and hear whether or not that behavior contravened secular law.

The Japanese not only punish themselves by experiencing strong feelings of shame when they do something they regard as wrong, they are also subject to a variety of sanctions by others around them, over and above any law, adding to their sense of shame.

Since punishment for misbehaving in a shame culture is first of all self-inflicted and immediate, shame is generally more effective in controlling the behavior of people than spiritual-oriented guilt feelings, which can be downplayed or denied altogether.

While Confucianism may have provided much of the foundation and framework of Japan's shame culture, the Shinto-based emotional content of their culture added enormously to the power of shame to motivate and control them.

Spirituality

The Japanese have never been religious in the Western sense of this term. But until modern times they were among the most spiritual of all people. They regularly followed precise customs and rituals to keep themselves in harmony with nature and the spirit world.

Today, the spiritual foundation of Japanese culture has been pushed into the background, but it is still there in the hearts of the older generations, and is still acknowledged on special occasions by the young. And there are signs that more and more Japanese are rediscovering the importance of the spiritual side of life—not as preached or practiced in the organized religions of the world, but as a part of their culture.

Some of the spiritual wisdom that a growing number of Japanese are returning to is found in Shinto, their ancient indigenous religion, which has been covered over by the popular culture of the West. But it is still there in the subconscious of the people, waiting to be revived.

The ancient Japanese, like other ancient people, recognized and understood the physical and spiritual relationship between man, the Earth and the cosmos far better than those whose view of the world and man's place in it became distorted beyond reason by Judaism, Christianity and Islam.

A full-fledged revival of the positive elements of Shinto would put the Japanese ahead of much of the rest of the world in spiritual terms, and provide an example for people worldwide.

Organized religions of the West and Near East are, in fact, gradually disappearing and being replaced by individual efforts to connect with the spiritual dimension of life and the cosmos. The more educated people become in the societies dominated by Christianity, Judaism and Islam and the more individual freedom they achieve, the more rapidly these cult-religions will fade away.

Style
The right-brain orientation of the Japanese and the resulting feminine orientation of Japanese culture has made the Japanese especially style conscious and provided them with the ability to create refined, pleasing forms and styles.

This mindset and ability applies across the board in all areas of Japanese life, and is especially conspicuous in the arts, crafts, interior decorations, house wares, and more—including such mundane things as wrapping paper and shopping bags.

The style of Japanese things is distinguished by their aesthetic appeal and by a sensuality that derives from their form, the materials used, and the harmonious use of colors and decorations. A lacquered jewelry box, for example, that combines the richness of black lacquer flaked with silver and gold has a beauty that transcends the materials it is made from.

By using the left side of their brains to conceive of articles that have practical, commercial value, and then bringing the right side of their brains into play in the designing and finishing of the product, the Japanese are able to create products that are both beautiful and saleable.

In Summary
It goes without saying (to use one of my favorite Japanese sayings) that the world would be a much better place if people in left-brained cultures became more aware of the advantages of using both sides of their brains.

[END]

*The author's other books on the mindset and culture of the Japanese are available from book stores, Amazon.com, BarnesandNoble.com, and other online booksellers.